THE PROBLEM WITH

EARLY NAVIGATION TOOLS

BLOOPERS OF INVENTION

oOPs!

BY RYAN NAGELHOUT

T0014653

Gareth Stevens
PUBLISHING

Please visit our website, www.garethstevens.com. For a free color catalog of all our high-quality books, call toll free 1-800-542-2595 or fax 1-877-542-2596.

Library of Congress Cataloging-in-Publication Data

Nagelhout, Ryan.
 The problem with early navigation tools / Ryan Nagelhout.
    pages cm. — (Bloopers of invention)
 Includes bibliographical references and index.
 ISBN 978-1-4824-2776-9 (pbk.)
 ISBN 978-1-4824-2777-6 (6 pack)
 ISBN 978-1-4824-2778-3 (library binding)
 1. Navigation—Juvenile literature. I. Title.
 VK559.3.N45 2016
 623.89028'4—dc23

                                        2015014563

First Edition

Published in 2016 by
Gareth Stevens Publishing
111 East 14th Street, Suite 349
New York, NY 10003

Copyright © 2016 Gareth Stevens Publishing

Designer: Sarah Liddell
Editor: Ryan Nagelhout

Photo credits: Cover, p. 1 Hadel Productions/E+/Getty Images; p. 5 Fred Stein Archive/Contributor/ Archive Photos/Getty Images; p. 7 Anton Watman/Shutterstock.com; p. 9 Rama/Wikimedia Commons; p. 11 (main) Hulton Archive/Staff/Hulton Fine Art Collection/Getty Images; p. 11 (Icelandic spar) ArniEin/Wikimedia Commons; p. 13 (main) Brian Maudsley/Shutterstock.com; p. 13 (Polaris) John A. Davis/Shutterstock.com; p. 15 (sextant) Scorpp/Shutterstock.com; p. 15 (drawing) Morphart Creation/ Shutterstock.com; p. 17 Triff/Shutterstock.com; p. 19 (map) Steven Wright/Shutterstock.com; p. 19 (cartographer) Photo Inc/Science Source/Getty Images; p. 21 Alexey Boldin/Shutterstock.com.

All rights reserved. No part of this book may be reproduced in any form without permission in writing from the publisher, except by a reviewer.

Printed in the United States of America

CPSIA compliance information: Batch #CS15GS: For further information contact Gareth Stevens, New York, New York at 1-800-542-2595.

CONTENTS

Words in the glossary appear in **bold** type the first time they are used in the text.

FINDING THE WAY

People are usually thought to have five senses: smell, sight, taste, hearing, and touch. But we actually have many more senses, such as heat and pain. One of the more interesting senses we may have is a sense of direction.

For thousands of years, humans have used things to better find their way around. They've used many wild machines to **navigate** our world. They had to make sure these things were **accurate**, otherwise they could get lost!

OOPS!

Scientists say a human's sense of direction can get better over time. You have to pay attention, or you can get into trouble!

SUN AND STARS

The first tools used by humans to navigate can still be used today—you just have to look up! For thousands of years, people have used the position of the sun throughout the day to figure out where they're going.

The sun rises in the eastern sky in the morning. At midday, it sits overhead, and in the afternoon, it begins to set in the western sky. However, the position of the sun does differ based on where you are on Earth.

OOPS!

At night, some sailors followed the stars or moon. However, they noticed these all moved in the night sky. This made it hard to follow without newer tools to track them.

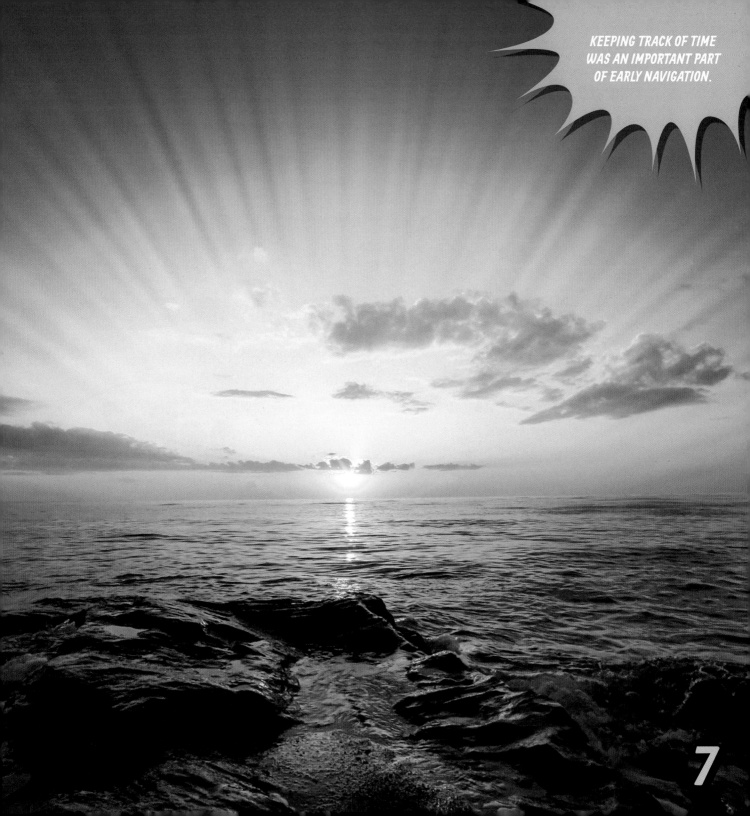

THE LEAD LINE

Traveling by ship was tough in ancient times. One of the earliest navigation tools simply kept boats from running aground. Called a lead line, it was a long length of rope with a weight at the end that sailors dropped into the water.

The lead line measured ocean depth, helping sailors keep track of how much water was under a boat. Water depth was measured by fathoms, or lengths of 6 feet (1.8 m). The lead line was mentioned by the Greek historian Herodotus in the fifth century BC!

OOPS!

The weight on the bottom of English lead lines in the 1600s was 7 pounds (3.2 kg). This is half a "stone," a weight measurement equal to 14 pounds (6.4 kg) used today.

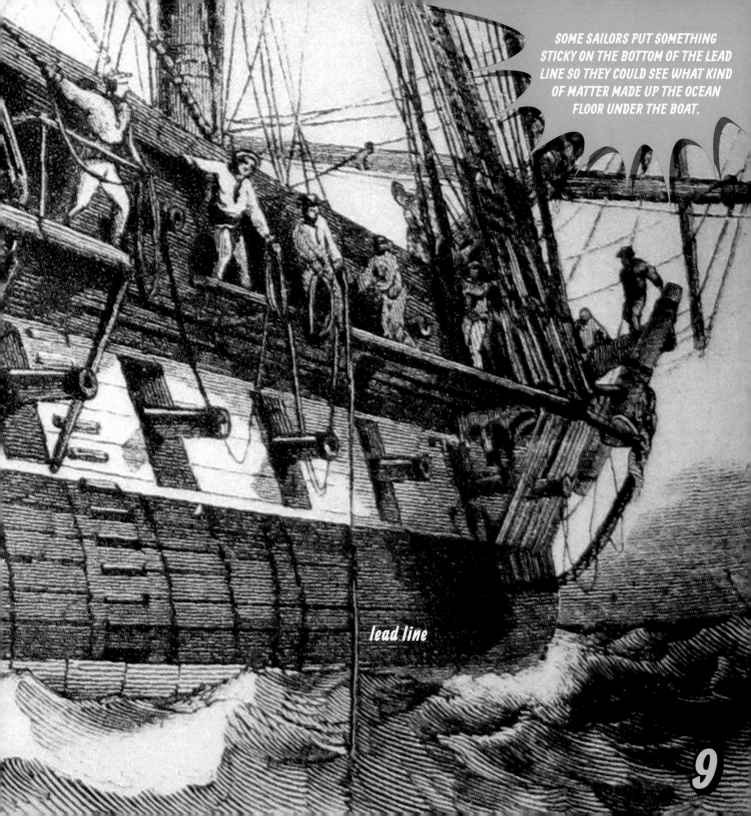

SOME SAILORS PUT SOMETHING STICKY ON THE BOTTOM OF THE LEAD LINE SO THEY COULD SEE WHAT KIND OF MATTER MADE UP THE OCEAN FLOOR UNDER THE BOAT.

lead line

9

VIKINGS ON THE WATER

The Vikings were a group of people who lived in Scandinavia starting around AD 700. They attacked other people's land by traveling on ships. Vikings had people specially trained to navigate on water. They also brought birds on their ships when they sailed. The birds were released over the water, and the ships followed them back to land.

Researchers think Vikings used crystals to navigate on cloudy days. One, called Icelandic spar, would change color when it turned in the light. This is how they found the sun through the clouds!

OOPS!

Many people think the first trips across oceans were accidents! Ships were blown off course by wind and storms, or a navigator called a helmsman may have made a mistake.

Icelandic spar

SCANDANAVIA IS A REGION OF NORTHERN EUROPE MADE UP OF MODERN-DAY DENMARK, NORWAY, AND SWEDEN.

USING THE ASTROLABE

Many sailors used the North Star, or Polaris, to navigate. They started to make tools to find and use stars more accurately. The astrolabe was one of the earliest tools to measure the **altitude** of stars to correct a ship's movement. Legend says the Greek thinker Hipparchus first invented it.

The astrolabe hung **perpendicular** to the water. Sailors then lined up the light from the star through the pinholes to measure the altitude of a star such as Polaris compared to the **horizon**.

OOPS!

Movement caused by wind or rough waters made it tough to use the astrolabe. Measurements made at sea could be off as much as 5 degrees, or 300 miles (483 km)!

IF THE ASTROLABE IS TILTED TO ONE SIDE WHEN USED, THE ANGLE WON'T BE ACCURATE. THE USER HELD IT BY STICKING A FINGER THROUGH A RING AND LETTING THE ASTROLABE HANG TO KEEP IT STRAIGHT.

Polaris

13

AND LATER, THE SEXTANT

The sextant is a more accurate type of measuring tool similar to the astrolabe. It uses mirrors to reflect light from the sun and find the sun's angle. John Bird made the first sextant in 1759.

Sailors pointed the sextant's first mirror at the sun, then moved the vertical piece forward or backward until the light **reflected** off the two mirrors and through the eyepiece. Navigators used the sextant with their charts and tables to figure out where on Earth they were so they didn't get lost!

OOPs!

The first sextant was so big and heavy it needed to be held up by a support to be used. The support piece sat on the user's belt so they didn't have to lift its whole weight!

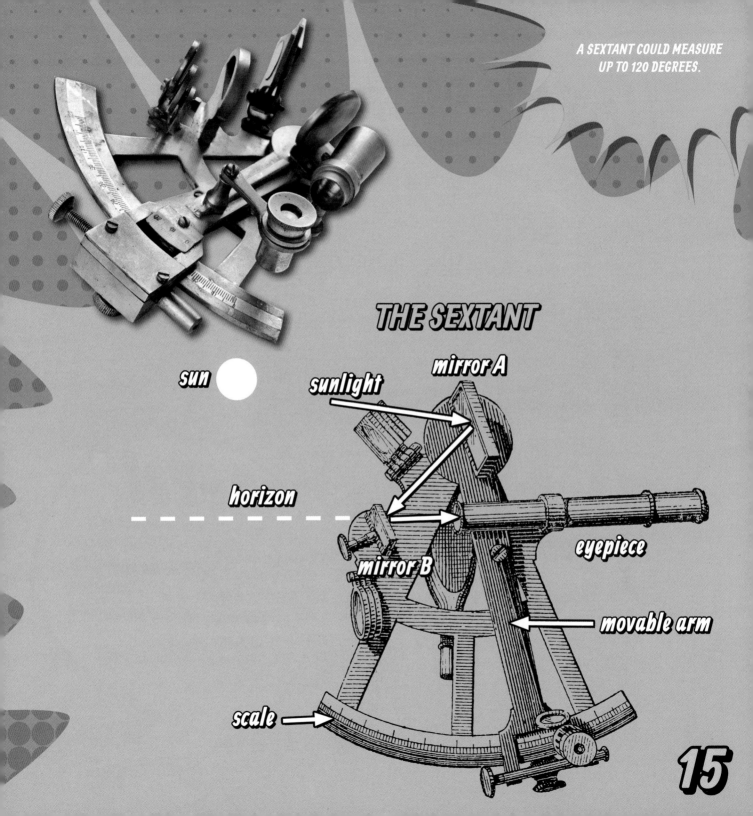

THE SEXTANT

sun

sunlight

mirror A

horizon

mirror B

eyepiece

movable arm

scale

USING MAGNETS

Magnets could be used to navigate because they point to the North or South Poles. In 1040, a Chinese writing described "an iron fish" that hung in water and pointed south. This was the first compass!

The problem with early compasses was that magnetic north, where a compass needle actually points, is not the geographic pole, or "true" north. Someone traveling from east to west with an early compass had to track the difference between the two points to stay on course.

OOPs!

The difference between true and magnetic north actually changes from place to place on the planet! This made navigating in bad weather very hard because sailors always needed to remeasure the difference between the two points.

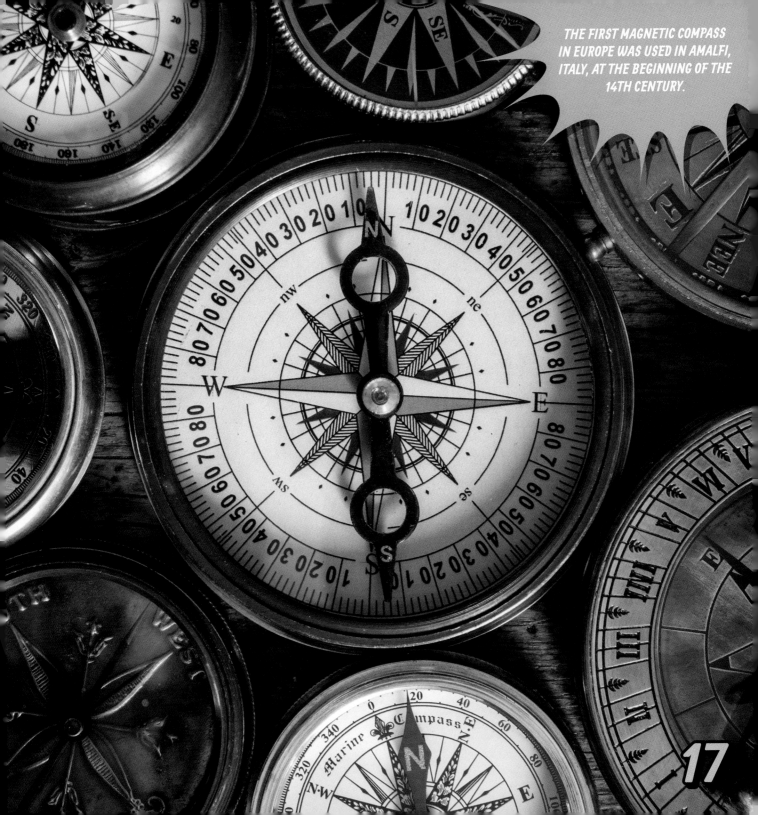

THE FIRST MAGNETIC COMPASS IN EUROPE WAS USED IN AMALFI, ITALY, AT THE BEGINNING OF THE 14TH CENTURY.

BAD MAPS

A cartographer is someone who makes maps. Early maps were made by people trying to chart just what the world looked like from above. They would explore new areas, drawing what they found and adding to or updating existing maps.

Few early maps were perfect. Some 17th century European maps claim that the state of California is an island! Others show the wrong size for different things. One map shows Greenland and Africa as the same size, but Africa is about 14 times larger!

OOPS!

Cartographers could only map places that were already known. If they hadn't been explored, parts of the map were left blank!

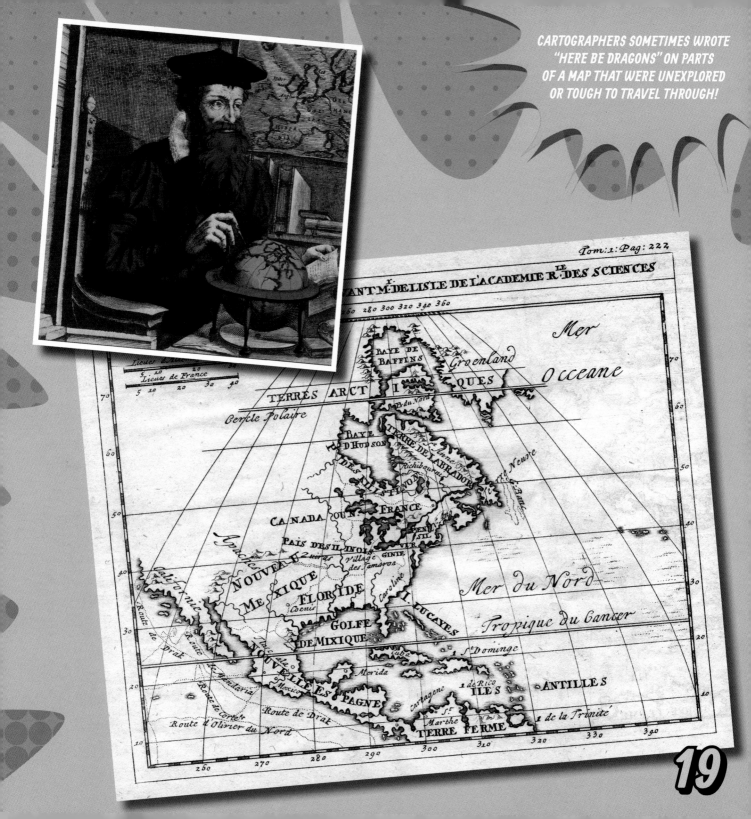

CARTOGRAPHERS SOMETIMES WROTE "HERE BE DRAGONS" ON PARTS OF A MAP THAT WERE UNEXPLORED OR TOUGH TO TRAVEL THROUGH!

19

GPS

Global Positioning System, or GPS, uses a series of **satellites** that orbit, or move around, Earth. A device like a cell phone gets in touch with these satellites to pinpoint where you are on the planet.

Even GPS isn't perfect. If you're underground or in certain areas, it may be hard to reach the satellites needed to make it work. Even today, navigation systems can fail, and people can get lost.

OOPS!

The US government used GPS in the 1960s and 1970s and didn't start sharing it with others until a Korean passenger jet was shot down by the Soviet Union in 1983.

STUDIES HAVE SHOWN THAT
USING A GPS SYSTEM CAN ACTUALLY
HURT A PERSON'S SENSE
OF DIRECTION!

21

GLOSSARY

accurate: free from mistakes

altitude: the height of something above the horizon line

global: relating to the entire world

horizon: the line where the earth or sea seems to meet the sky

navigate: to make one's way over or through

perpendicular: exactly upright, or forming a right angle with another line

reflect: to give back light

researcher: one who studies to find something new

satellite: an object that circles Earth to collect data or aid in communication

FOR MORE INFORMATION

BOOKS

Dickinson, Rachel. *Tools of Navigation: A Kid's Guide to the History & Science of Finding Your Way.* White River Junction, VT: Nomad Press, 2005.

Morrison, James E. *The Astrolabe.* Rehoboth Beach, DE: Janus, 2007.

Prentzas, G. S. *GPS.* Ann Arbor, MI: Cherry Lake Publishing, 2010.

WEBSITES

Explorers at Sea: Navigation Tools
cccoe.net/lifeatsea/student/navtools.htm
Learn more about the tools explorers used on boats here.

Navigation
education.nationalgeographic.com/education/encyclopedia/navigation/
Discover more ways people navigate our world on this National Geographic site.

Publisher's note to educators and parents: Our editors have carefully reviewed these websites to ensure that they are suitable for students. Many websites change frequently, however, and we cannot guarantee that a site's future contents will continue to meet our high standards of quality and educational value. Be advised that students should be closely supervised whenever they access the Internet.

INDEX